Boss Presence
~~100~~, ok ~~50~~, ok Some Tips for We Bad Chicks To REIGN at Work

by

Dawn R. Rosemond, Esq.

To M.B.D.M., my why! I love you!

Jordan,

First, great haus! I thank you for thinking enough of me to involve me. You are so impressive. You KF 16N!

Dawn

Rock H.

Dawn

Hair/Makeup: Toni Irby, Owner, Upgrade Salon and Custom Glory
Wigs
Photographer: The EYEDEA Studio
Publisher: AJ Publishing

Contents

WARNING

By reading this book, you are expressly and unequivocally accepting the following as your truth and promising to walk in said truth going forward:

1. You're a 'bad chick!' Not bad, bad. But Michael Jackson, bad! Michelle Obama, bad! Wonder Woman®, bad (both Linda Carter and that new one that showed up in *Batman vs. Superman: Dawn of Justice*)! Whether you've arrived or are still asking for directions – whether everyone knows you or you're still waiting on an introduction – you are still standing, still showing up, still fighting. You're a bad chick!

2. You were created to REIGN! To what? Yep! To REIGN as in you are royalty. The word REIGN literally means to conquer, to ascend, to rule, dominating power, to wear a crown, to win. One source[1] defines REIGN as the 'essence of win.' Anyway, that's why you're here. God said so (*see* Romans 5:17; Psalm 8:1-9; Genesis 1:28 just to name a few)! And if you are honest with yourself (regardless of your beliefs), you know

so. Like when you're down and something inside compels you to rise. Or, when you "know, that you know, that you know," as my momma says, that you were made for "more" even though you are currently rock'n "less", those aren't pipe dreams – you're not crazy – greatness is hardwired into your DNA. That's your royalty calling!

Introduction

It is difficult today to talk about leadership or even attend any leadership conference, without there being some discussion about this 'thing' called executive presence. No one truly knows what executive presence is, but purportedly, it is something you must have to get ahead — to get promoted — to win. Women and minorities purportedly do not have it as much as our white male counterparts. Wrong. Forbes Magazine[2] defines executive presence as, "the ability to project gravitas — confidence, poise under pressure and decisiveness," or the 'it' factor. Fortune Magazine[3] contends it is, "part charisma, part gravitas, with a dash of the ineffable." My kids simply call it 'boss,' which I have come to learn means: incredibly awesome, great, excellent, preeminent, 'mad fly'. You're "boss". Since you are still with me (still reading), you own this truth about you, even if you have no feelings to back it up. *See* WARNING (*i.e*, the page you just read).

So, *Boss Presence* is not an endeavor to tell you what

executive presence is, and then convince you that you need to get it to win. You already have it; you have already won! (Again, *see* WARNING). According to Dr. Al Jennings, best-selling author of, *God's Not Mad At You: He's Madly In Love with You*[4], and *Basic Training For Victorious Living*[5], "We are not fighting to win, we are fighting from win." Thus, Boss Presence is an endeavor to share some of what I have learned, gleaned, and peeped out in my 20+ year career to hopefully help you, challenge you, and inspire you — my fellow 'bad chicks' — to rock your royalty and REIGN the way that you were intended, both at work and beyond.

CHAPTER ONE
Be What You Needed

It is invaluable when you can find yourself in the success that you desire — to see others like you, conquer the very mountain you are about to climb. Unfortunately, such models of achievement often do not exist, especially as a woman of color. This was my truth. When I began practicing law in 1996, there were no other black female lawyers in my firm. And while there had been black female lawyers before me, none had ever made partner. I will not lie to you and say that this void consumed me, as I was then (and remain) primarily focused on being an excellent lawyer and servant to my clients. But I distinctly remember times longing for someone to call who could answer my mundane, (but potentially career-altering) questions like, "should I wear my hair natural or straight?" And when I became a capital partner in 2005 — our firm's first-ever — I remember longing for someone to show me how to be at the table in this body — in this skin — with this flow.

Please do not misunderstand me. There are some 'bad chicks' I get to call my colleagues, my partners, whom I glean from daily. I have had, and continue to have, amazing mentors and champions throughout my professional journey: men, women, black, white, alike. One does not have to look like you to be for you. But a void existed for me nonetheless.

Roughly five years ago, I encountered what I thought was some type of mid-life crisis. I know now that it was my royalty calling me. The greatness inside of each of us is without repentance. Much will be required of you. Change most of all. Anyway, I was whining profusely about the meaning of my life, and whether anything I was doing mattered at all. I was frustrated with God for not answering me fast enough and with having to wait. So I whined. Of course, the whining worked, and now I am writing this book. The End. Please! No, instead, I whined and got 'tuned up.' Proverbs 3:12 provides, "It's the child He loves that God corrects." Man, that dude loves me, 'cause all I got by way of direction was: stop whining about your purpose, and what you are to become, and 'be' what you needed to those around you — both to the black female attorneys walking the journey you began now 20 years ago and beyond. Be the mentor, the sounding board, the support, the example you longed for — you'll find your purpose there in your selflessness.

I bet that's where yours is hiding. Plainly, I suspect you are reading this because you have dreams of your greater self. I bet you've even seen glimpses of 'her.' But if she's like mine, that chick is elusive and seems at times, so far off. You can focus on that distance or choose life — that is, choose the opportunity right in front of you to draw her near.

Regardless of where you are in your career journey, someone is watching you — someone needs you just as you are right now. They need you to answer their questions, to tell them that they are not their mistakes, to affirm their royalty. Be what you needed (indeed, what you may need right now). You may have no feelings to back it up; in fact, you may be wondering how you give from a depleted place. But it is this action that will

fill you up and open you up to your next best self.

CHAPTER TWO
Pull Up a Chair

So let's be clear — your invitation was not lost in the mail. You did not miss a meeting. Say it with me — you were not invited to sit down. I join Facebook COO, Sheryl Sandberg, in her directive to the working woman — "Sit at the table."[6] Screw the invitation. Just pull up a chair. Not because you have no respect for their limits. But as a 'bad chick' who REIGNS, you just simply cannot adopt their perceived limitations of you as your own. Indeed, you have to decide that the limitations others place on you have nothing to do with you. One who did not create you cannot legitimately weigh in on your worth and value.

So pull up a chair. Volunteer to lead the team. Apply for the job. Enroll in that class…in that school. Raise your hand. Have an opinion, an idea, and then voice it. If you are not heard, or if you're offering was interrupted mid-stream, say it again. Say it louder.

Time to be clear again. Pulling up that chair and taking a seat at the table will cost you. The price — your excellence. According to Mahatma Gandhi, "Speak only if it improves upon the silence." Translation for our purposes: don't speak, don't move, don't get in the game if you haven't handled your business. Please know, I am not tacitly ratifying those studies that show that women don't typically move unless they are 100% (sometimes 120%), certain they can 'do it,' while men tend to engage at around the 40% confidence level. I am not talking about perfection. Shooting for perfection ends in self-marginalization. But showing up at the table less than excellent makes you purposefully mediocre, and that ain't cool either.

I don't watch a lot of television, but I love ABC's hit reality show Shark Tank. It's made for TV, so it's a bit dramatic. But I dig creativity on display, and I am a consummate student, so I love the mini business school lessons that are shared each week. It always amazes me when people show up in the Tank with amazing ideas or inventions, but completely fall apart when asked normal questions like what were their sales last year, or what are their margins, or what are their plans to scale? I get that they are there because they need a Shark's help, but there is no excuse for not knowing the basics about their own business.

So it is with you — with me — with we 'bad chicks' who REIGN. I desire to be on a paid board. I need to increase my financial acumen. I'm taking courses and otherwise studying to that end. You want to start your own business? Research what you need to know about your industry. Talk to other entrepreneurs. Read up on entrepreneurship and what it takes. You desire to be a part of your company's leadership team? Make sure you know your company's business as best you can — not just the part attached to your current assignment. Bottom line, "Raise your hand before you are qualified. Don't wait for an invitation to make a difference," as said by Carey Lohrenz, first fully-qualified female naval aviator to fly the F-14 Tomcat in the United States Military. Your excellence however, is the difference maker. Don't you dare sit down without it.

CHAPTER THREE
Work Like a Girl

Okay, so if you have never seen the *Always* commercial spot (#LikeAGirl), stop right now, go pull it up and watch it. It's transformative. Powerful. Necessary. I remember when I first started practicing, taking inventory of other women professionals just to assess how to be. I recall feeling confused because for all of the talk about breaking barriers, what I observed were women making great strides for women, but acting like men. Their suits were really just men's suits with a skirt. Their speech, akin to any men's locker room. And their efforts to downplay the beauty of femininity (*e.g.*, bearing children, raising them, wanting to get home to be with them), constant. Indeed, the very word 'girl' was deemed a bad word even though that is exactly what we are; I think it's still considered negative when referencing a grown woman.

Now I get it. Along with that lost invitation to sit at the table is often a visceral reaction to us having the audacity to show up in the boardroom, in the courtroom, etc., female (or a

person of color, or different in any respect). So I fully

understand the need to do what you have to do to get what you

want — what you deserve. I have nothing but respect for the

hustle of those who have gone before me. But I see opportunity

here.

As is reflected in the *Always* spot, why can't doing

something "like a girl" also mean winning? Good news — it

does (you already know, *see* WARNING). So, wear dresses or

suits that fit you. Put on makeup, get your nails done, keep your

hair tight. Wear pretty shoes and rock cool purses. Cry. Yep, I

said it. Cry. Now, on this one, you should maybe wait until you

are in your office behind closed doors, or on a bathroom break.

Breaking down in front of your superiors I've heard is frowned

upon; okay, I've done it. It is frowned upon. That said, we are

emotional creatures, and acting like we are not, or that being

emotional is a weakness, serves no one. I have been a practicing

lawyer for two decades. The practice of law is sometimes like a prizefight with Mike Tyson (in his prime) on the other side. I

suspect you can say the same regarding your respective gig.

Anyway, as one would expect in such a fight, sometimes them

blows hurt. Sometimes they knock the very wind out of you,

such that tears are the only reasonable response. Tears,

however, do not compromise your strength. Just don't get stuck

in them. Further, recognize that when you are done crying, you

will still have to face the issue that produced them in the first

place. So let it out. Feel. Be in the moment. Then deal.

Dominate. Hit back.

Finally, know this, I am not trying to set women back.

Further, I am not attempting to limit what it means to be a

woman. I get that we are all so vastly different. So, if you don't

like dresses and wear your nails short and natural, no worries.

No need to write me. I am simply saying, if we are going to be

the proverbial 'only one in the room,' be the only one in the

room. And in doing so, make it clear to all, that your presence at

the table, in all your 'girly-ness,' is a value-add. Indeed, it's a game-changer.

CHAPTER FOUR
Be Kind

There is a scripture in Luke 6:35-36 that directs me. It reads:

"I tell you, love your enemies. Help and give without expecting a return. You'll never — I promise — regret it. Live out this God-created identity the way our Father lives toward us, generously and graciously, even when we're at our worst. Our Father is kind; you be kind."

We all have a brand whether we are actively working on it or not. A brand is not a logo. It's what you deliver consistently — not from your perspective, but from the perspective of those who encounter you.

A few years ago, I was challenged to ask 5 to 10 people who know me what they think of me, or rather, what do they think my brand is. Scary question, with potentially scarier answers, right? Anyway, as I think about what I want people to say about me, and what they did say about me, I settle on this one thing — I want my brand to be: Dawn is kind. When I work with her, she is kind. When she deals with clients, she is kind. When she corrects me or directs me, she is kind. When she is corrected or directed, she is kind.

By definition, the word kind means, "of a good or benevolent nature or disposition, as a person; indulgent, considerate, or helpful; humane." You would think being such would be an obvious notion. I mean, it's a part of the 'golden rule,' or at least implied by it. But I have come to learn that there are many highly educated, highly paid, highly skilled, 'high enough to know better,' people who act as if they totally flunked kindergarten. At times, unfortunately, I have been one of them. I have treated someone trying to learn from me like they were their mistake. Or I have failed to extend grace to someone in a situation in which grace was previously extended to me. The result: harm to them and to the content of my character.

So, I've made a conscious decision to come up higher. I challenge you to do the same. It will cost you nothing. Scratch that. It will cost you everything, because the decision to be kind, especially when kindness is not being afforded to you, is the quintessential 'road less traveled', or the 'rough side of the mountain,' or whatever phrase is most appropriate to convey the sucky, doesn't feel good path. But developing a brand of kindness will also position you for everything: more clients, more opportunities, more money, promotion, exposure. We have settled that you are a 'bad chick' who REIGNS. So, if your career or business opportunities are seemingly stalled, I encourage you to check your brand.

CHAPTER FIVE
Quit

Quit! Quit? Yes, quit! Quit making excuses. As my beloved Sorors of Delta Sigma Theta Sorority, Incorporated taught me, "...they are the tools of the incompetent." Quit being late to work. Quit being late period. It is the height of disrespect and it brands you as not worth the investment.

Quit complaining. There is no life in it, and it changes nothing. As Maya Angelou once said, "If you don't like something, change it. If you can't change it, change your attitude. Don't complain."

Quit planting mediocrity (*e.g.*, resting or playing when you are supposed to be working, doing 'just enough' because 'more' don't translate into more dollars), and expecting greatness. Light has no communion with darkness. To be mediocre[7] means to be 'inferior', 'second-rate', 'barely adequate.' For a bad chick who REIGNS, mediocrity is midnight.

Quit believing what 'they' say. You know, the 'they' who is

never defined, yet an authority on everything. 'They' said you

couldn't make it. 'They' said you aren't smart enough. 'They' said

that no other woman has ever tried to do what you want to do.

'They' told me I would be a 'C' student because of a poor

showing on my SATs. Got A's and B's all four years. 'They' told

me I wouldn't pass the bar my first time because of the color of

my skin. One and done. 'They' told me there's no way I'd get a

job and certainly, no way I'd still be welcomed after five years.

Blessed with 20 years practicing so far – at the same place I

started.

My point, 'they' lie to you, and to me. 'They' can't help it

because their very existence is grounded in our fears – fears of

our perceived inadequacy or known greatness. Both can be

equally debilitating. Bottom line, we can never rise any higher

than our beliefs about our self. It's hard enough getting those

right without 'they' commenting. Stop giving them mugs a voice.

Finally, quit quitting on you. Life is hard. The journey for

one who dares to flow with difference, even more so. But you were built for hard. What does that mean? To REIGN also

means, "to overcome" or "to superabound." *Overcome* means,

"to be victorious, to come out on top; to get the better of in a

struggle or conflict." And *abound*[8] means, "to be rich or well

supplied." Can you tell I love words? Can you tell my social life

as a kid was...special? I digress.

So if you and I were created to REIGN (the belief of

which you clearly understand now is a prerequisite to you vibe'n

with me), then what you are saying about you – no, believing

about you – is that regardless of the situation, you were

positioned from jump to emerge victorious with an uber

portion of riches and wellness. Translation: Baby, you were built

for hard. So quitting on you is the ultimate 'bad bet' because by

definition, you and I are a sure thing.

CHAPTER SIX
Bless Your Food

My momma is a follower of Christ; she always has been. As such, she raised my brother and I to pray before we eat. Nothing fancy – just you know, "Thanks God for this food. Please let this really be chicken and regardless, don't let anything in it kill me." I cannot say definitively that I understood the 'why' behind praying over ones food when I was a little girl. But as I have grown literally, and in my relationship with God, I not only understand why my mom trained us this way, but now count it an absolute privilege to open my mouth and say thank you for having food to eat, water to drink and nourishment for my body. To me, that's just what followers of Christ do. In reality (or rather in my experience), that's what followers of Christ do *outside of work.*

That is, I cannot tell you how many times I've witnessed said followers relegate blessing their food during a business meal to a weird grunting sound made while simultaneously shoving food into their mouth; that is, assuming they endeavor to pray over their food at all. I'm ashamed to admit it, but I used to be such a tepid creature. It was when I first started working. Remember, I did not know how to be. And even though I had been a follower of Christ in my own right for some years (in fact, since I was a teenager), I didn't think I had to worry about it at work because I didn't think He was there. Now that I think about it, my past suggests that I didn't think God accompanied me to college or law school either; and He certainly can't see in Mexico.

Anyway, I remember not knowing whether to pray or when. What if my colleagues or clients think I'm weird? What if they're talking to me (which was typically the case)? Is it rude of me to interrupt? What if they don't believe what I believe, so they find my praying offensive? I never got answers to these questions. Not sure I ever really sought them out. All I know is that I came to a place where I no longer cared, and made a promise to God (and to myself), that I would never soft-peddle

Christ nor downplay His hand on my life.

So to my fellow followers, whether alone or with the CEO – whether having a casual business meal or one that could alter your career, bless your food! Per Bishop T.D. Jakes in his teaching series and best-selling book *The Ten Commandments of Working in a Hostile Work Environment*, "You are there to be a light." You are there to reflect His goodness, not by preaching it, but by living it. You are there to be His representative. You are there (whether you like the job or not), to change a culture.

Please know, I totally understand the concept of separating 'church and state,' or in this case, 'church and work.' But a true follower of Christ cannot lay down their beliefs anymore than wet can be separated from water. So bless your food! Shine! Light is useless under cover. And to my non-followers who hung in there with me through this – thank you for your patience. Your takeaway: the next time we have lunch, just give me a few minutes.

References

[1] www.urbandictionary.com

http://bit.ly/1WHFKBh

[2] October 29, 2012 Forbes Magazine article by Jenna Goudreau, Forbes Staff- "Do You Have 'Executive Presence'?

[3] June 5, 2014 Fortune.com article by Anne Fisher: Can 'executive presence' be learned?

http://for.tn/1uQStlu

[4] God's Not Mad At You: He's Madly In Love with You, Dr. Al Jennings

http://amzn.to/1WHvJE5

[5] Basic Training For Victorious Living, Dr. Al Jennings

http://amzn.to/1rlLidN

[6] January 18, 2011 Forbes Magazine article by Carol Frohlinger, Contributer-- Sheryl Sandberg On Why Women Need To 'Sit At The Table'.

http://onforb.es/1VmKeOg

[7] www.dictionary.com

http://bit.ly/1SyuqHD

[8] www.dictionary.com

http://bit.ly/244dvyI

[9] Ten Commandments of Working in a Hostile Environment, T. D. Jakes

http://amzn.to/25KEkMy

About Dawn

Dawn R. Rosemond is a partner in the law firm of Barnes & Thornburg LLP, an AmLaw 100 firm. She works out of the firm's Fort Wayne, Indiana office where she serves as the administrator of the Litigation Department and is also a member of the firm's Pro Bono and Legal Personnel committees. Dawn is the first black female partner in the firm's history and is reportedly the first black female lawyer to matriculate from associate to partner in the State of Indiana.

In conjunction with her legal practice, Dawn serves as a deliberate mentor to young lawyers, other young professionals (both within her firm and beyond), and students of all ages, with a particular heart for championing women and young girls. She has also developed and launched *REIGN*, a leadership platform tailored to everyone. Through this platform, Dawn hosts 'vibe sessions' (as she calls them), and talks entitled *REIGNtables*™, and *REIGNclass*™, respectively, each centered around her staunch belief that regardless of the challenges we may face, we were all created to reign in this life.

Among many other accomplishments, Dawn is an Indiana Torchbearer Award recipient -- the State of Indiana's most prestigious recognition of women in Indiana. Dawn has also been named one of the most influential African-Americans in Northeast Indiana by INK Magazine®. She is a proud member of Delta Sigma Theta Sorority Inc., and an even prouder wife and mother of two boys. Through a series of lasting content, including her upcoming app *REIGNdrop*™, Dawn's purpose is to reign as she was created to do -- to live a life 'poured out' -- while convincing the world that they were created to do the same.

Made in the USA
San Bernardino, CA
07 January 2017